Savannah

Hostess City of the South

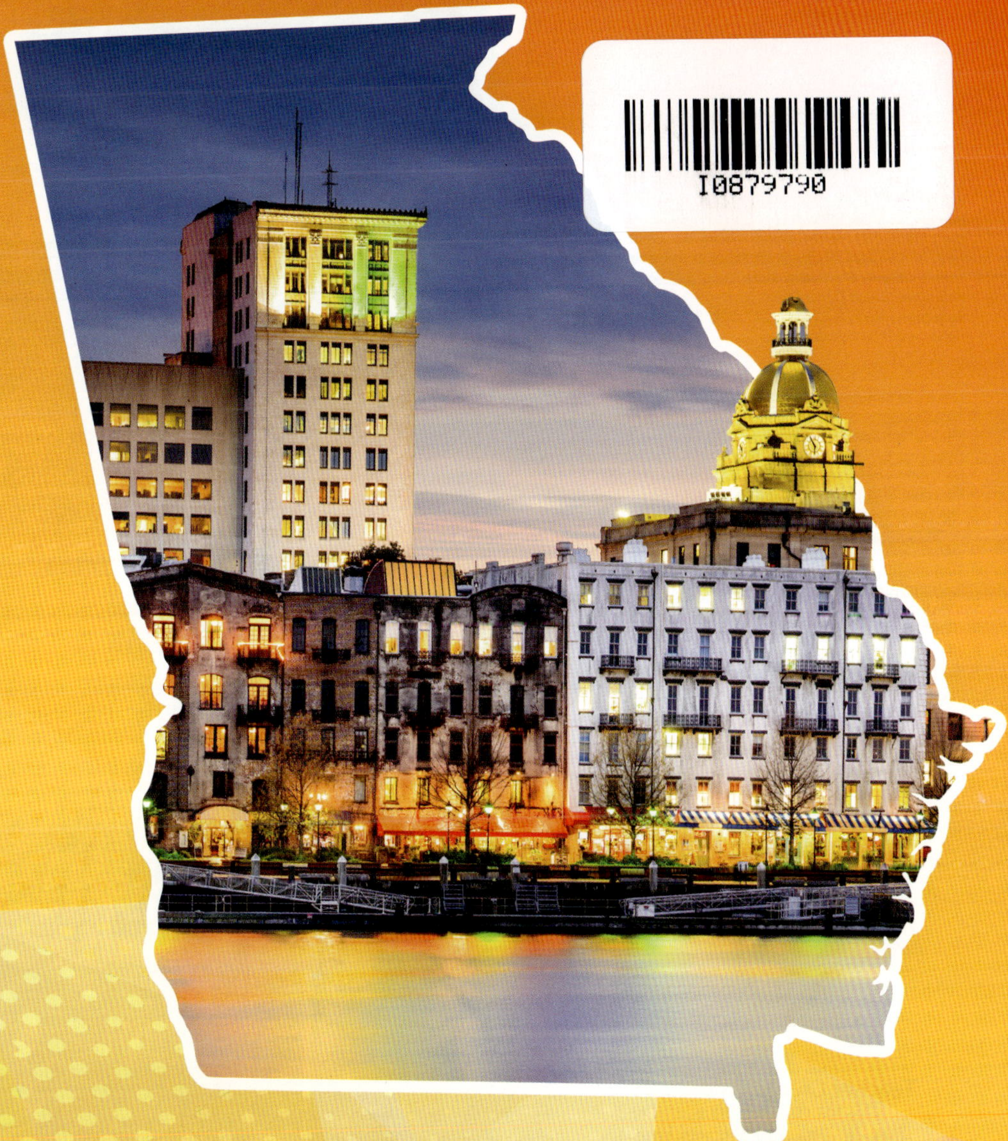

Katelyn Rice

Consultants

Regina Holland, Ed.S., *Henry County Schools*
Christina Noblet, Ed.S., *Paulding County School District*
Jennifer Troyer, *Paulding County Schools*

Publishing Credits

Rachelle Cracchiolo, M.S.Ed., *Publisher*
Conni Medina, M.A.Ed., *Managing Editor*
Emily R. Smith, M.A.Ed., *Series Developer*
Diana Kenney, M.A.Ed., NBCT, *Content Director*
Torrey Maloof, *Editor*
Courtney Patterson, *Multimedia Designer*

Image Credits: pp. 2,4,6,15,16,17,18,32 North Wind Picture Archives; p.6 LOC [G1019 .R6 1808]; pp.6-7,9,10-11,12,19,21 Granger, NYC; p.4 Bob Pardue - Georgia / Alamy Stock Photo; p.8 Courtesy of Ed Jackson; p.10 Everett Collection Historical / Alamy Stock Photo; pp.17,20 Buyenlarge/Getty Images; p.22 Handout/ Handout/Getty Images; p.25 Blend Images / Alamy Stock Photo, p.25 Frances Roberts / Alamy Stock Photo; pp.27,31 Garry Gay / Alamy Stock Photo, Corbis; p.28 Cultura Creative (RF) / Alamy Stock Photo; p.29 Bert Hoferichter / Alamy Stock Photo, Ian Dagnall Commercial Collection / Alamy Stock Photo; All other images from iStock and/or Shutterstock.

Library of Congress Cataloging-in-Publication Data

Names: Rice, Katelyn, author.
Title: Savannah : hostess city of the south / Katelyn Rice.
Description: Huntington Beach, CA : Teacher Created Materials, 2016. |
Includes index. | Audience: Grade K to grade 3.?
Identifiers: LCCN 2015042497 | ISBN 9781493825585 (pbk.)
Subjects: LCSH: Savannah (Ga.)--History--Juvenile literature. | Savannah
(Ga.)--Juvenile literature.
Classification: LCC F294.S2 R53 2016 | DDC 975.8/724--dc23
LC record available at http://lccn.loc.gov/2015042497

Teacher Created Materials
5301 Oceanus Drive
Huntington Beach, CA 92649-1030
http://www.tcmpub.com

ISBN 978-1-4938-2558-5

Printed in Malaysia
Thumbprints.24705

Table of Contents

Welcome to Savannah! 4
A Colony Begins 6
Building Savannah 12
Savannah at War 18
Growth and Change 22
Savannah Style 26
Plan It! 28
Glossary 30
Index 31
Your Turn! 32

Welcome to Savannah!

Do you know which Georgia city is the oldest? It is Savannah! It was founded in 1733. It sits on the banks of the Savannah River. It has homes and parks. There are businesses there, too.

The city gets a lot of rain. It is humid there. This means the air is wet and damp. The summers are hot. But many people love living there. There are things for locals and **tourists** to do. That is one reason why people visit this city. They like the beauty and history there, too.

Savannah in 1734

Southern Hospitality

Hospitality means "to treat guests with warmth and good manners." People in the South are said to be known for their hospitality.

A Colony Begins

Can you imagine leaving your home and moving to a new place? Long ago, many people left their homes in Europe (YOOR-up). They moved to the New World.

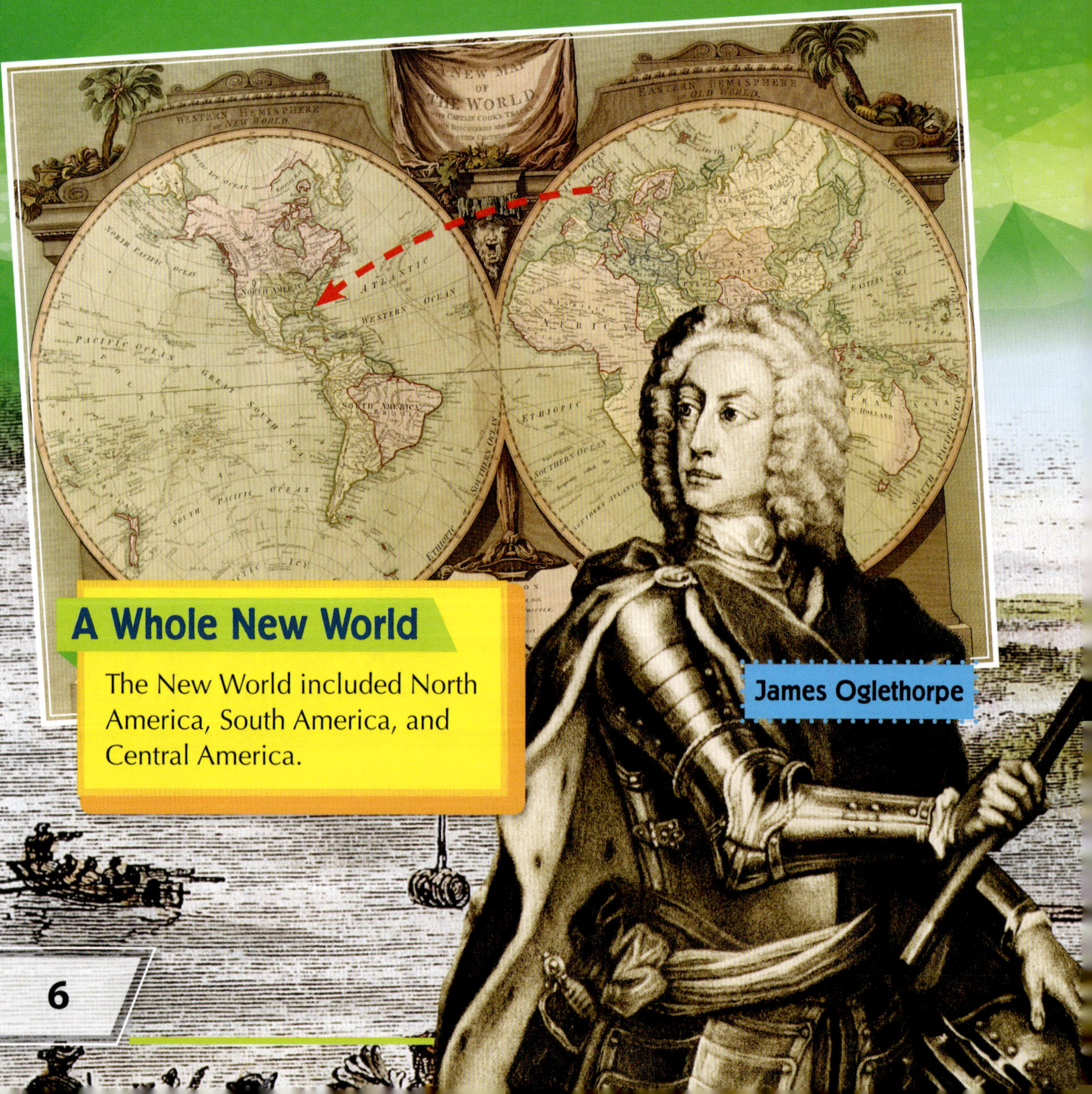

James Oglethorpe

A Whole New World

The New World included North America, South America, and Central America.

In 1732, James Oglethorpe set sail for the New World. He sailed on a ship called the *Anne*. **Settlers** came with him. They sailed to the new **colony** (KAHL-uh-nee) of Georgia. They arrived two months later. James and the settlers wanted to build a new town. They found a nice spot near a river. They called their new town Savannah.

Colonists arrive in the New World.

American Indians were already living in the area. James wanted to tell them his plan for the town. But he did not know their language. And the chief did not know English. Mary Musgrove was there to help!

Mary's father was British. Her mother was an American Indian. She was taught both languages. She helped the two men talk to each other. They signed a **treaty**, or a deal. It meant James could start building his new town.

Mary Musgrove

Birth Name

Coosaponakeesa (KOO-sah-puh-nay-KEE-suh) was Mary Musgrove's birth name. It means "Lovely Fawn."

James Oglethorpe meets with Tomochichi, the chief of the tribe.

This map shows Savannah around 1796.

Savannah was made to be an orderly town. James used 24 squares to make a grid. And 22 of the squares are still there! The town had wide streets. It also had a lot of parks. This gave people a place to meet and talk. They could do business. Or they could talk with friends.

Changing Laws

At first, slavery was against the law in Georgia. But the founders changed the law in the 1750s. Slavery was legal in Georgia.

James also helped write laws for the Georgia colony. Some of these laws were different from those in other colonies in the New World. One such law said that people could not own **slaves**.

Building Savannah

The colonists worked hard to get the new town of Savannah started. They cut down trees. They used them to build houses. They planted gardens. They tried to grow the food they had in Europe. But it was not easy. The soil was not the same in the New World. They had to learn how to grow new kinds of food.

The climate was different, too. The weather was hot and humid in Savannah. There was a lot of rain. But the people did not give up. After much hard work, Savannah was built.

Trying New Things

The colonists had to learn to like new food. They tried sweet potatoes and maize, or corn, for the first time in Georgia.

Colonists build Savannah.

The life of a colonist was not easy. There was not enough food for everyone most of the time. They were often hungry. There were lots of new illnesses. But there were no cures. They often got sick.

Colonial children had a hard life, too. They had to work and help their families. They helped with farming, cooking, and cleaning. Sometimes, boys went to school. Or they learned at home. Girls did not get to go to school. They had to help take care of the younger children and do other chores.

A colonial girl churns butter.

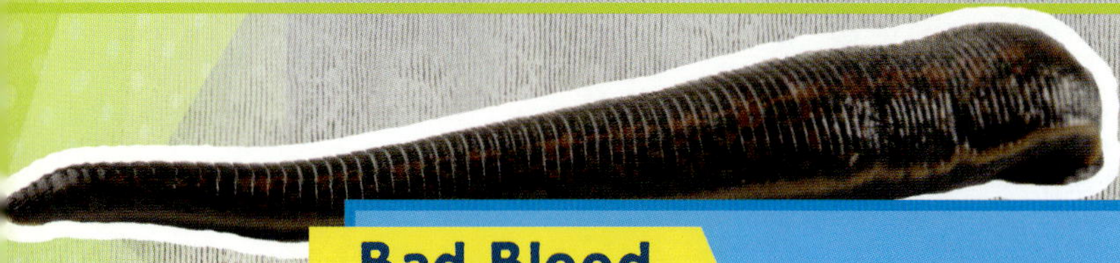

Bad Blood

Colonial doctors used leeches to drain people of "bad blood." They thought blood was the reason someone was sick. Leeches sucked the "bad blood" away. Many people died.

A colonial boy attends school.

a plantation house

colonial money

Colonists in Savannah had different jobs. Many were farmers. Some had small farms. Others had big farms. These were called **plantations**. Some colonists were **merchants**. They sold goods at local shops.

Savannah is a port city. That means it is a city close to the ocean. It has a place for boats to sail in and out with goods. Many colonists had jobs at the port. Some were sailors. Others were traders.

This map shows Savannah in 1779.

Savannah at War

Years later, the colonists were ready for a change. They wanted to be free. They did not want the British to rule them. This started the American Revolution. The colonists fought the British.

Savannah was seized during the war. It was taken over by the British. They were in charge of the town for four years. They used its port for their ships. But the colonists won the war in 1783! The United States was born. Georgia was no longer a colony.

The British attack Savannah in 1778.

Save the Date!

Georgia officially became a state on January 2, 1788.

This 1864 map shows General Sherman's attack on Savannah.

In 1861, the Civil War began. This war was between the North and the South. The states in the north wanted to **abolish** (uh-BAHL-ish) slavery. They wanted it to end. The states in the south wanted to keep their slaves. Georgia fought for the South.

General William T. Sherman

President Lincoln

General Sherman and his troops move through Georgia.

Merry Christmas, Mr. President!

General Sherman told President Lincoln he captured Savannah as a Christmas present for him.

General William T. Sherman fought for the North. He was going to set all of Savannah on fire! But he changed his mind. No one knows why. Some say it was because he thought Savannah was too pretty to burn.

In 1865, the South lost the war. Slavery ended.

Growth and Change

Today, more people live in Savannah than lived there in the past. Life in the city is much easier than it used to be. There is medicine to help people who are sick. And all children go to school! It is still very hot in Savannah. But people learned how to cool their homes. There is still a lot of rain. Sometimes, there are hurricanes! But people know how to stay safe in the storms.

A hurricane passes over Savannah.

Savannah then

Savannah now

Long ago, colonists had to grow their own food. But they could not grow enough. Many were hungry. Today, people do not have to grow their own food. They can buy it at a store. Or they can go to a restaurant.

Savannah is known for good food. Fresh seafood is often on the menu. Crab stew is a well-liked dish. Have you heard of "soul food"? Fried chicken and fried okra are both types of soul food. Many people visit Savannah just to eat!

Savannah Style

Many people like to visit Savannah. Some take tours of the city. Tour guides take them around town. They show them all the sites. The guides tell them the history of the city.

Savannah has parks and museums. You can take a riverboat cruise. You can ride a trolley through the old town. Or you can look for dolphins in the ocean! The city is full of fun things to see and do. Savannah may be the oldest city in Georgia. But it is as beautiful today as its founders hoped it would be.

Girl Power!

Juliette Gordon Low started the Girl Scouts. You can visit the house where she was born. It's on Oglethorpe Avenue in Savannah!

Plan It!

Pretend you and your family are planning to visit Savannah for a day. What would you like to see or do? Would you visit a museum or go to an old military fort? Would you try new food or take a tour? Write a plan for your trip.

SAVANNAH
MUSIC
FESTIVAL
ACCESSIBLE
ENTRANCE

Glossary

abolish—to officially end or stop something

colonists—people living in an area that is ruled by another country

colony—an area ruled by a faraway country

hospitality—being friendly to visitors and guests

merchants—people who buy and sell goods

plantations—large farms that produce crops for money

settlers—people who go to live in a new place where there are few other people

slaves—people who are forced to work without pay and have no freedom

tourists—people who travel for fun and pleasure

treaty—a deal that is made between two or more countries or groups

Index

American Indians, 8

American Revolution, 18

Civil War, 20

colonists, 7, 12–14, 16–18, 24

Europe, 6, 12

Lincoln, Abraham, 21

Low, Juliette Gordon, 27

Musgrove, Mary, 8

New World, 6–7, 11–12

Oglethorpe, James, 6–11

plantations, 16

settlers, 7

Sherman, William T., 20–21

slavery, 11, 20–21

Your Turn!

Chores Then and Now

Colonial children had many chores. This girl is churning butter. This was probably only one of her many chores. What chores do you do at home? How do you help? Write a list of the chores you do in a week.